MW00985642

Eyes on Jesus
Daily Devotions for Lent and Easter

Lisa M. Clark

CONCORDIA PUBLISHING HOUSE • SAINT LOUIS

Ash Wednesday
and the Days Following

Misjudging Eyes

Read Mark 14:3–9

But Jesus said, "Leave her alone. Why do you trouble her? She has done a beautiful thing to Me." (Mark 14:6)

When we see Jesus, what do we see? Is He our teacher? a healer? our guest at the dinner table? Yes, He is, just as He was all those things to the people who were visiting with Simon the (former) leper in the reading for today's devotion. But He is much more than that.

A woman saw Jesus and knew what He was going to do: He was going to die; and she honored Him in the best way she knew how. She came with costly perfume and offered it to Him, anointing His head.

When we see other believers, what do we see? The disciples and others gathered that day saw a foolish woman who wasted good money. But Jesus saw a woman with wisdom beyond her peers, for she freely gave Him her love and devotion.

"She has done a beautiful thing to Me." Jesus honors this woman in a beautiful way, ensuring that we still would read of her deed. He promised the others, "What she has done will be told in memory of her" (v. 9).

Lord Jesus, forgive our misjudging eyes, which forget who You are and forget others who love You. In Your name we pray. Amen.

To See Perfection

Read Genesis 1:26–31

And God saw everything that He had made, and behold,
it was very good. (Genesis 1:31)

It was good. It was very good. Those words might seem ordinary to our ears, but there was nothing ordinary about what God saw when He looked upon His completed creation. It was very good. It was perfect and whole.

Have you ever seen perfection? Think about it. What is the most amazing, most beautiful, most awe-inspiring thing you have ever beheld?

It wasn't perfect.

Adam and Eve had seen perfection in the paradise God had made for them, but with their sin, all of creation fell. Rocks, trees, animals—all fell under the curse that came with sin.

Now, our vision is imperfect. We see a sin-filled world with sinful eyes.

Even when God watched His very good creation fall subject to death, decay, and destruction, He saw the end. He knew that He would send His Son to become like His creation in order to redeem it. More than that, He would restore it. There will come a day, God promises, when He will make a new heaven and a new earth.

On that day, we will see perfection, and it will be very good.

Lord of Creation, look at me through the promise of resurrection and restoration. Keep my eyes focused on the day when I will see You and all things made perfect. Amen.

Eye Opener

Read Genesis 3:6–7

Then the eyes of both were opened.
(Genesis 3:7)

Have you ever had an eye-opening experience? This kind of event can be any time you suddenly realize something you didn't before. Sometimes that's a good thing. You learn a great lesson. You gain a special insight. Sometimes that's a bad thing. You realize that someone had been lying to you. You learn of a terrible truth.

Adam and Eve thought that they wanted their eyes to be opened. They wanted to be like God, knowing the things He knew. And what did they learn?

They learned that they were naked. They learned that they were not God. They learned that they had made a terrible, horrible, irreversible mistake. Maybe Adam and Eve suddenly wished they could undo, unknow, unsee what they had done.

But it was too late. And now, we often see more than we want. We see pain, death, suffering, anger, and all kinds of evil.

Jesus sees it all too. He saw it all as He endured it all on the cross. He has seen every sin that you have ever done, and there is nowhere to hide it. It's all laid bare.

And because Jesus saw it all, and paid for it all, He now sees us as forgiven. Holy. Redeemed. That is an eye-opening truth that fills us with joy.

Lord Jesus, open our eyes to see Your love and Your mercy. Amen.

Look toward Heaven

Read Genesis 15:4–6

Look toward heaven, and number the stars.
(Genesis 15:5)

Some of us may not be able to see the stars between all the buildings and streetlights. Others of us may see stars so often that we don't think to look up and gaze at them with wonder anymore.

When was the last time you looked up at a sky full of stars and marveled at the Creator who made them?

Abraham looked up at those stars thousands of years ago, and God Himself spoke. God promised Abraham a family of descendants that would outnumber the stars. Even more than that, One in Abraham's line would make the children of Abraham the children of God.

In Jesus, born in the line of Abraham, all who believe in God are numbered with Abraham's descendants—and there are more of us than there are stars in the sky.

So the next time you look at the stars, think of God, who had the power and creativity to make them. And also think of all your brothers and sisters in Christ, who are so many they would outshine the heavenly bodies with the light of God's Word to a darkened world.

Lord Jesus, You fulfilled the promise to Abraham when You were born. And we are a part of that promise too. Help us to shine as stars with Your light. Amen.

LENT
WEEK ONE

See, I Must Suffer

Read Matthew 16:21–23

From that time Jesus began to show His disciples that
He must go to Jerusalem. (Matthew 16:21)

We sometimes try to shield our eyes from difficult truths. We turn off the news report. We scroll past the breaking news. We look away from the homeless person sitting on the bench.

It can seem too much to bear sometimes. We just can't handle all the bad news, the sad stories, the painful realities.

But Jesus sees it all. He knows it all. And He carries it all on His shoulders.

Jesus told His disciples that He was going to Jerusalem. He told them that He was going to suffer. He told them that He would die and then rise.

But His disciples didn't want to listen. Peter, in fact, scolded God Himself!

We, His disciples, do the same, don't we? We ignore the suffering. We hide our hurt. We tell God He doesn't know what He's doing when we ignore His Word, when we plug our ears to the suffering of others, when we tell Him that all the hurt in this world is His fault.

And Jesus sees it all. He knows it all. And He carries it all—even our sins against Him—on His shoulders. He then takes it to the cross and defeats it all with His death and resurrection.

Lord Jesus, forgive us when we refuse to see all that You've done for us. Help us to see what You did for all on the cross and help us to show others. Amen.

NO EYE HAS SEEN

Read Isaiah 64:1–4

From of old no one has heard or perceived by the ear, no
eye has seen a God besides You. (Isaiah 64:4)

No one. Not a single one. Not a single time.

Never once has someone called on another god and found healing.

Not ever has someone prayed to another god and received deliverance.

No time in history has someone witnessed another god intervening for the sake of humankind.

But our God does. He has. And He will.

He is the God who delivered His people from the slavery of Egypt, and the slavery of sin.

He is the God who rescued His people from enemy armies, and the enemy Satan.

He is the God who redeemed His people from exile, and from the sentence of eternal death.

In Jesus, we see the God who loves the unlovable, saves the condemned, and restores the helpless.

Even so, we seek after other gods. We look to our money, our safety, our health, our government, and ourselves—forgetting that every one of these things is merely a gift from the one and only God.

This Lent, take some time to name the false gods you trust in. Can they save you? No, of course not. Then pray to your God, the one who hears you, the one who loves you, the one who promises to forgive you.

Triune God, You alone are Lord. Forgive me when I turn to false gods; hear me when I pray to You. Amen.

God Has Revealed

Read 1 Corinthians 2:7–10

These things God has revealed to us through
the Spirit. (1 Corinthians 2:10)

I can only imagine.

It's a common phrase that describes something so amazing that
only imagination could begin to try to understand it.

But our Bible passage today talks about things we can't *even* imagine. "No eye has seen, nor ear heard, nor the heart of man imagined"
(v. 9). What is it that we can't imagine? "What God has prepared for
those who love Him" (v. 9).

And yet, God reveals His plans for us. The Spirit searches the depths
of God (Can you imagine?) and comforts us. The Spirit, who lives in us,
teaches us and leads us to anticipate the amazing mysteries of what God
is preparing for us.

This side of Jesus' return, we still can't comprehend what will happen when only joy and beauty and love exist. But what we do know is
enough to give us hope through Lent, through suffering, and throughout all of life as we wait for the day when we see God with our own eyes.

Lord Jesus, we can't even imagine all that You have done and will
do for us. Thank You for sending Your Spirit to us to reveal such joy
as we wait for You. Amen.

BETRAYING EYES

Read Mark 14:10–11, 18–21, 41–46

[Jesus said,] "Rise, let us be going; see, My betrayer is at hand." (Mark 14:42)

Jesus knew. He knew exactly who His betrayer was. He knew Judas from the inside out. He knew his quirks, his preferences, his thoughts.

Judas thought he knew Jesus. His mission, His motives, what He should be doing with His newfound fame. But Judas didn't understand Him at all.

"Rise, let us be going," Jesus said. If we knew our betrayer and the scheme against us, most of us would do something about it. We would stop him. We would escape. Our call to "rise" would be to rise up in arms or to rise up and leave. Jesus took action—but it was to play right into His betrayer's hands. Why? Because it fit inside His ultimate plan to save us all. Even people like Judas. Even people like us.

We betray Jesus with our sin, our selfishness, our schemes. Our eyes fail to see what Jesus is all about. But Jesus never forgot why He came to earth, and despite the grief that comes with betrayal, He stayed faithful to us and to His mission to save us.

Lord Jesus, forgive us when we betray You and when we fail to see Your plan. Thank You for never failing to forgive us. Amen.

Clearing the Log

Read Matthew 7:1–5

Why do you see the speck that is in your brother's eye,
but do not notice the log that is in your own eye?
(Matthew 7:3)

We tend to go to extremes, don't we? When it comes to others, we tend to do one of two things:

"It's my job to make sure everyone is doing the right thing, even if that means being harsh."

"Who am I to judge? Most things aren't that big of a deal. I'd rather keep my friends no matter what."

As usual, Jesus points to a better way. And He starts with a truth we've ignored: we have a log.

In other words, yes, of course our neighbor has a problem, a sin, an issue that is separating him or her from God. And so do we. Our denial of our problem makes it even worse! So get rid of that log.

Why? So we can be better than the others? So we can let the others live with their specks? No. Jesus shows the practical purpose of seeing ourselves clearly. Now, we can help our neighbor with his or her speck, so we're both better off. How might that look?

No matter how the conversation looks in your own situation, you know that Jesus sees both you and your neighbor with eyes that don't miss a log or a speck. And He also sees both you and your neighbor with eyes that don't fail to forgive.

Lord Jesus, forgive us, that we may serve others. Amen.

In His Sight

Read Psalm 51:1–6

[I have] sinned and done what is evil in Your sight.
(Psalm 51:4)

David wrote Psalm 51, and he wrote it after learning an important truth: God sees everything.

To summarize, David broke a commandment and then every single other commandment in a domino-effect of sin. And he thought he got away with it all.

But God confronted David, through Samuel, out of love and righteousness. David's sin separated him from God, and God intervened.

We, like David, think we can get away with our sins. We assume no one will ever know. But God confronts us, through His Word, out of love and righteousness. Our sin separates us from God, and God intervenes.

God sees everything. That can be a terrifying thought, except that our God is loving. Jesus loves us so much that He took all those sins—every single one of them—and paid for them when He died on the cross. Now we, like David, can confess our sins in repentance. And God sees our sins no more.

Lord, You see my sin, and You forgive it all. Thank You for Your love. Create in me a clean heart, O God, and renew a right spirit within me. Amen.

BEHOLD, A GREAT MULTITUDE

Read Revelation 7:9–10

I looked, and behold, a great multitude that no one
could number. (Revelation 7:9)

John was given a unique opportunity: a vision of what life will be
like with God forever. And what did he see? People. Lots and lots of
people.

It can be easy to forget sometimes that life forever with God also
means life forever with all who call upon His name. What an incredible
celebration that will be! We get to live together in peace, joy, and holy
love. We'll get to behold the glories of God all together with people of
every nation, and we'll be able to do so without any divisions, barriers,
or conflicts.

Look around your community. What divisions are there? Pray to
God for help in healing relationships now in anticipation of and witness
to the everlasting relationship we'll enjoy together with Him. As you ob-
serve your community, are there others who need to hear God's Word?
Pray also to God for help in sharing His Good News of salvation with
others, that they, too, may be numbered with the multitudes.

Lord of all nations, help me learn from brothers and sisters in
Christ from other nations as I, too, share Your saving message to all
in my midst. Amen.

LENT
WEEK TWO

A Light to My Path

Read Psalm 119:105

Your word is a lamp to my feet and a light to my path.
(Psalm 119:105)

Has any of the following ever happened to you?

You're walking down a hallway, and someone suddenly turns out the lights.

You're on your way back from a hike, but the sun is setting faster than you anticipated.

You drive out on a rural road on a moonless night. You park in the middle of a field and cut the headlights.

Darkness changes a path. Even if you know a road fairly well, a path looks different without a light to guide.

Without the light of God's Word, our path is bleak. We might think we know the way, but it's easy to veer off track, to trip over a branch, to encounter another creature lurking in the shadows. It's impossible to see all the danger, and fear of the unknown can be paralyzing.

But the Word in our lives illumines the way, and the darkness scatters from us. We can see clearly what lies ahead, and we can trust God to lead the way.

How often do you read God's Word? Thank God for the gift it is in your life, and pray for a heart that seeks His Word daily.

Heavenly Father, thank You for the gift of Your Word, which points us to Jesus. Thank You for Your Son, the Word made flesh, who leads the way to eternal life. Amen.

WHERE TO LOOK

Read Micah 7:7–8

But as for me, I will look to the Lord. (Micah 7:7)

In a popular detective show, a woman was hiding something important. The detective was able to find out its location by faking a crisis. In her panic, the woman looked straight at her treasure's whereabouts.

In a panic, where do you look? In a crisis, where do you turn?

In our sin, we often look in the worst places. We look to the danger, distracted by its power. We look to a quick fix, assuming that we can try to escape disaster without facing it. We look to ourselves—even though we're usually the ones who caused the problem in the first place.

There is only one place to look.

The Lord sees all the danger. He knows all the problems. He is more powerful than all the enemies of sin, death, the devil, and our sinful nature.

Our eyes only need to focus on one place: on our Lord, whose focus is on rescuing us from all danger.

Lord Jesus, fix my eyes on You every day. Keep me in Your love and care. Amen.

Birds and Flowers

Read Matthew 6:25–34

Look at the birds of the air: they neither sow nor reap
nor gather into barns, and yet your heavenly Father
feeds them. (Matthew 6:26)

Look at the birds. Go ahead. See if you can find a bird nearby. There are birds all over, but we often overlook or ignore them. God doesn't. He sees them. He feeds them. He cares for them.

Look at the plants. How many days go by that you pass the grass, fields, and gardens without noticing their beauty? God doesn't forget the flowers or trees. He adorns them with intricate colors that proclaim His creative power.

God sees the birds. He notices the plants. Why would He possibly forget about you?

Take a cue from the birds and sing a song of praise. Take a cue from the flowers and witness to the God of creation. And rest secure, knowing that God sees, knows, and loves you. He sent His Son to die for you. He will come back for you. And He will take care of you, now and forever.

Lord Jesus, help me see the birds and plants, and remind me that I am in Your care. Amen.

WATCH AND PRAY

Read Mark 14:32–42

Remain here and watch. (Mark 14:34)

It can be too much. Jesus asks for us to watch and to pray and to be ready. But what do we do? We fall asleep.

We fall asleep, forgetting the urgent need to share the Gospel.

We fall asleep, ignoring the invitation and need to pray.

We fall asleep, denying the importance of time with our Savior.

This is a dark world, brothers and sisters. Liars and deceivers wait to silence Jesus. They try to attack us. Will we fall asleep when there is so much at stake?

The disciples did. And we do too.

Guess who doesn't sleep. Jesus. Guess who still does pray for us. Jesus. Guess who is eagerly preparing for the Last Day. Jesus.

We fail, and Jesus forgives. More than that, He gives us strength so that we can indeed watch and pray and prepare for the day when He comes again, gathering us to Him forever.

Lord, forgive us when we fall asleep. Thank You for always keeping watch for our sake. Amen.

A Night of Watching

Read Exodus 12:40–42

It was a night of watching by the Lord. (Exodus 12:42)

The Israelites were bound in slavery, and God heard their cries for rescue. He brought about an epic exit, in which two million people walked out of the land of their oppressors toward a land God promised to them.

And as they walked out, the Lord kept watch.

What a powerful image to think about. It's a big trip with lots of people and belongings. Plus, there was the danger that the Egyptians would suddenly attack as entire families walked the streets at night. But the Lord kept watch and ensured deliverance after the first Passover.

Almost fifteen centuries later, a Passover like no other was taking place. The Lamb of God would sacrifice His own life, and His blood would cover the sins of the world. God kept watch as Jesus walked right into the bondage of the Romans and the chains of sin so that we would be able to walk away, free to enter the promised land.

And the Lord kept watch.

Every moment of Jesus' last moments before death was carefully orchestrated, fulfilling countless prophecies of the Messiah and conquering the horrible oppression of Satan. It was an epic exit for us, as we were set free.

Lamb of God, You shed Your blood to save us all. Keep watch over us as we await the day we see You in the promised land forever. Amen.

First Things

Read Psalm 5:2–3

In the morning I prepare a sacrifice for You and watch.
(Psalm 5:3)

First things first.

There is a popular speech that's been going around social media for a while now. The advice is to make your bed at the beginning of the day. The idea is that making your bed is a great way to accomplish something early in the morning.

Not a bad idea.

Here's another great idea (it comes from God): pray. The passage above talks about a "sacrifice." Filling your morning with prayer frames your day with conversation with your God. It could be before breakfast. It could be while making your bed. Regardless, we are called to pray to our Lord, and we can watch throughout the day as our God watches over us.

There's something funny about watching through the eyes of prayer: we begin to see our day in the context of the prayers we offer to the Lord, and we begin to pray in the context of what we see throughout the day. We watch and pray; we pray and watch.

Blessings on your watching and praying today. Your loving Father promises to hear your prayer for the sake of Jesus Christ, who speaks on your behalf as you pray.

Father, hear our prayer. Savior, speak for me. Spirit, guide my prayer. Amen.

I Lift Up My Eyes

Read Psalm 121

I lift up my eyes to the hills. From where does my help come? (Psalm 121:1)

Look up. What do you see?

If you're in the city, you may see tall buildings.

If you're in the mountains, you may see tall, rocky peaks.

If you're in the heartland, you may see sky everywhere.

When the Israelites looked up, they saw idols.

Psalm 121 is a song people would sing on their way to Jerusalem. They would climb their way up the long incline to the city of David. And all around them, shrines with idols would stand tall on the hills.

While singing this psalm, people would look and see the hills. From where did their help come? Not from the idols, but from the God of all, whom they would worship once they were in Jerusalem.

Where do you lift your eyes? Where do you seek help? Are your idols able to protect you? From where does your help come? Only from the God of all, who went to Jerusalem to redeem us from all.

Lord Jesus, lift my eyes to You, and help me in my time of need. Amen.

LENT
WEEK THREE

In the Sanctuary

Read Luke 11:14–23

I have looked upon You in the sanctuary, beholding
Your power and glory. (Psalm 63:2)

When you worship in church this week, pause wherever you look. What do you see?

That squirmy child? That's a believer whom God loves and invites into His presence. She's learning about Jesus' love through you and others.

That font? That's a portal that connects you to Christ Himself. He died and rose. You will too. Oh, and it also gives life, faith, forgiveness, and all kinds of other blessings.

Do you see that hymnal in front of you? Your brothers and sisters have written it for you, filling your heart, mind, and mouth with words of truth about God's love. Jaroslav, Anna, Paul, Elisabeth, Martin, and Ambrose are just a few of them. (Who knows? Maybe the young man behind you will add a few to the list someday.)

How about that pulpit? God's Word will reach you with promises and truth and love and comfort today. Soak it all in; you'll need all that strength and wisdom for the week to come.

Oh, the bread and wine? Yes, and so much more. There's Jesus' real presence in body and blood so that you can touch your Savior and receive His forgiveness every time you commune.

That empty pew? Nah. This congregation is united with the Church Triumphant, where you join with angels and archangels and all the company of heaven (Grandma too) in praising God.

I could go on, but how about you take it from here? Behold God's power and glory in His sanctuary.

Lord, as I enter Your house, let me see all that You do for me in this place. Amen.

Lion on the Loose

Read 1 Peter 5:7–10

Be sober-minded; be watchful. Your adversary the devil prowls around like a roaring lion, seeking someone to devour. (1 Peter 5:8)

I can picture it now. On the evening news, a report goes out: "This just in! A lion is prowling around the neighborhood." Everyone's cell phones let out an alarm, giving the same information. Social media newsfeeds fill with comments about the incident.

Everyone would be watching for the lion.

So, why don't we? We have a lion in our midst, and he's the sneakiest kind. Sometimes he's doing his best when he lays so low that we forget he exists at all.

Oh, but he does. The devil hates God and hates everyone whom God loves (that would be everybody). So he lurks and prowls and stalks his prey, bent on devouring everyone he can before his time runs out.

If that doesn't sober your mind and make you watchful, I'm not sure what will. God warns us to stay alert and aware so that the devil cannot capture us.

Here's the good news. There's another Lion. They call Him the Lion of Judah. This Lion has already defeated the devil, and He protects us against all danger.

Yes, be watchful for that devil of a lion (lion of a devil?), but do not fear. The Lion of Judah, the Son of God, is watchful too, and you can turn to Him for all you need, including salvation.

Lord Jesus, protect me from the devil. Amen.

The Eyes of Your Hearts

Read Ephesians 1:15–18

[Have] the eyes of your hearts enlightened, that you
may know what is the hope to which He has called you.
(Ephesians 1:18)

There's a movie in which the main character is asked which pill he wants to take: one will show him the reality of his world; the other will make him forget everything.

What unfolds is a mind-bending reality for our hero, where he is both seeing the facade of his world and also seeing the reality of good and evil, bondage and freedom.

It's much like the Christian life. Sure, we can get distracted by the earthly things around us, lulled into a forgetfulness at all that truly surrounds us. But the more we hear and read and sing God's Word, the more our eyes become opened.

The fight with the spouse is also an attempt by the devil to taint what love truly means.

The person on the corner is also an opportunity to care for all of God's people.

The sleepy Sunday morning in is also a missed chance to see your family of faith and to be strengthened for the week ahead.

The eyes of our hearts know that even death itself is more than it seems. For the believer, it is a portal into victory and a rest until the resurrection.

With such an incredible vantage point, we can work in this world with an eternal purpose in all that we do.

Holy Spirit, open my eyes to remember that all I do is serving an eternal purpose. Give me all that I need to serve. Amen.

DENYING EYES

Read Mark 14:26–31, 66–72

And Peter remembered how Jesus had said to him,
"Before the rooster crows twice, you will deny Me three
times." And he broke down and wept. (Mark 14:72)

This is a heartbreaking moment for Peter, and for all Christians. Luke adds another detail: "And the Lord turned and looked at Peter. And Peter remembered . . ." (Luke 22:61).

Jesus knew it would happen. He knew Judas would betray Him. He knew His disciples would abandon Him. He knew Peter would deny Him.

Peter was determined in his shortsightedness. He couldn't see that he would ever trouble or leave or deny Jesus. But he caused trouble by striking Malchus's ear. He left Jesus in the garden. And he couldn't see past the moment when he went so far as to curse himself, denying his Lord, whom he had followed for years.

"Lord, to whom shall we go? You have the words of eternal life" (John 6:68).

"You are the Christ, the Son of the living God" (Matthew 16:16).

"I do not know the man" (Matthew 26:72).

Jesus knew it would happen. He knew Judas would betray Him. He knew His disciples would abandon Him. He knew Peter would deny Him. But He still loved them. And He still died for them.

He knew it would happen. He knew we would deny Him too. But He still loves you. And He died for you.

Lord Jesus, forgive me for all the times I deny You. Amen.

Eyes of Tears

Read Psalm 6

My eye wastes away because of grief. (Psalm 6:7)

The world is filled with tears. We cry in grief over loss. We cry in anger over conflict. We cry in fear over tragedy. We cry in loneliness, regret, sorrow . . .

Jesus cried too. In a world filled with sin, evil, and death, anyone dismayed over the fall will shed tears. And we have a God who mourns with us.

What hope is there? "The Lord has heard my plea; the Lord accepts my prayer" (v. 9). Our weeping can rise as prayer to our Lord, who listens and understands. More than that, He has done something about those tears.

Jesus died as the tears of His loved ones fell, and He rose, causing tears of joy for believers throughout the ages. When He comes back, He'll rid the world of all the sorrow and grief. And Jesus will wipe away every tear of our eyes.

Lord Jesus, thank You for listening to our tear-filled prayers. Thank You for the comfort You give. Amen.

Enlightening

Read John 19:7–9

The commandment of the LORD is pure,
enlightening the eyes. (Psalm 19:8)

We sometimes give the Ten Commandments (or any command) a hard time. We know we can't keep them. So as soon as we're told to, we hurry in with a "But we can't! We're sinners!"

Yes, that's very true. That's why we're so grateful for the Son of God who could do what we, as children, could not: keep the Law perfectly and fulfill it by satisfying the debt of our sins. We're free.

To do what?

Oh, right. We're free to follow God's commands—His will. Now, this is the joyful part: We don't follow God's commands because we have to for salvation. Instead, we get to follow them as children living without fear. We have no fear because we know we'll be forgiven when we fail. But we also take joy in God using us to serve our neighbors wherever He has placed us.

God's Law is a gift that enlightens His will for us. We don't have to guess at God's good pleasure; He tells us: "Love the Lord your God. Love your neighbor as yourself." In a word, *love*.

As beloved children, we love. Put another way, "We love because He first loved us" (1 John 4:19).

One of the best parts about following God's will is that when we do, we know we are serving as instruments, guided by the Holy Spirit, to enlighten those around us to the hope we have in Jesus.

Lord Jesus, use us as instruments of love and lights to the world. Amen.

SEARCHING FOR GOD

Read John 5:39

You search the Scriptures because you think that in
them you have eternal life; and it is they that bear witness about Me. (John 5:39)

People search for life in all kinds of places: healthy eating, unhealthy
eating, special memories, leaving a legacy, and more. At least the reli-
gious leaders of Jesus' day had it right that they should look to Scripture
for life. There was one problem: they didn't want to find life in Jesus.
They didn't want to find Jesus in the Bible. That's a problem, because
He's everywhere in the Bible, from the beginning to the end.

The Scriptures didn't change. The prophecies that clearly point to
Jesus cannot be ignored.

During this season of Lent, we have been blessed to spend time
in Scripture. Hopefully, you will continue to read the Bible throughout
the year. No matter what, if we are not seeing Jesus, we are missing the
point. Jesus is the answer to the sin we read about in Genesis. He is the
answer to the redemption that we see in the Gospels. He is the answer
to the restoration that we find in Revelation. The Spirit points to the Son
as we are reconciled to the Father.

Pray that the Word made flesh becomes apparent as you read the
Word for you.

Living Word, point me to Your truth and love. Amen.

LENT
WEEK FOUR

Let Your Light Shine

Read Matthew 5:14–16

"In the same way, let your light shine before others, so
that they may see your good works and give glory to
your Father who is in heaven." (Matthew 5:16)

"It's a great place to see and be seen."

This is a description given by the world about the trendiest, most famous hot spots. The idea is to gain attention for the sake of gaining attention.

It comes as a surprise, then, when God calls us to be seen. The difference is that we are not to be seen in the trendiest places, but often the lowliest. The difference is that we are not to be seen to gain attention for ourselves, but rather to point attention to God.

It's a strange thing, humility. Some don't care about it at all. Others believe that humility is denying that we have any gifts—but that is to say that God has not given us those blessings. True humility is recognizing that all good gifts—our talents, our works, everything—come from God and are for His glory

So, go ahead. Shine, especially in those dark, gloomy places. But as you do, remember that you are shining with reflected light so that others may look and see the One who gives you the light in the first place.

**Light of the world, shine Your light in me, that others may see
You. Amen.**

To See Jesus

Read John 12:20–22

Sir, we wish to see Jesus. (John 12:21)

They were Greeks, outsiders. At the time, the Jewish disciples wouldn't even consider eating with these Gentiles. They didn't associate with anyone who was not like them. But here these men were, seeking Jesus.

Does this happen today?

Maybe there are times when we ignore a newcomer at church.

Maybe we're hesitant to welcome a visitor who doesn't dress very well. We assume that the person just wants money.

Maybe we're concerned that if too many people come who speak a different language, it would mean work on our end.

Maybe we let fear get in the way of conversation as we're sure we'll get it wrong when talking about Jesus.

"We wish to see Jesus."

In a world where so many consider that Jesus is not for them, in a world where so many don't care about Jesus at all, it's a remarkable gift when someone requests to know about Jesus.

What will we tell them?

The beauty of the Last Day helps us remember that we have brothers and sisters who look and sound completely unlike us. We remember, too, that there are many who still wish to see Jesus.

Lord Jesus, thank You for loving all people. Help me to do the same. Amen.

Watching the Walk

Read Philippians 3:17–21

Join in imitating me, and keep your eyes on those who walk according to the example you have in us. (Philippians 3:17)

You can talk the talk, they say. But can you walk the walk?

There are plenty of people who claim to be believers. They say that they are a "person of faith." They might talk a great talk. But all too often, their walk gives them away.

They talk about love, but they are cruel to their neighbor.

They talk about patience, but they are quick to judge.

They talk about peace, but they stir up trouble.

And we do this too.

Any Christian knows that part of our "talk" is that we are all sinners. So while we know God calls us to show love, patience, and peace, we also know that we all fail.

So what does our walk look like then? Humility. Confession. Repentance.

Then, with the freedom of forgiveness, we walk the walk again.

Lord Jesus, forgive us when we fail to walk the walk or when we follow others who do the same. Restore us to a walk that is led by Your hand. Amen.

Murderous Eyes

Read Mark 14:1–2, 53–65

*And the chief priests and the scribes were seeking how
to arrest Him by stealth and kill Him. (Mark 14:1)*

There's a reason why the law puts more weight on premeditated murder.

All murder is wrong, of course, and subject to justice. But consider the cold, hateful, evil resolve to continually keep the death of someone else at the forefront of your mind.

Jesus was a wanted man, and there was nothing that could shake His enemies from Jesus' death. As terrible as that all sounds, there was an even stronger reason for Jesus' impending crucifixion.

There was nothing that could shake God from Jesus' death either.

As much as the chief priests thought that they were in control, as much as they truly harbored hate in their hearts, they were merely instruments of God's since the day Adam and Eve sinned.

Jesus was about to die on the cross for all sins, including the sins of those who would kill Him.

Have your eyes been murderous? You may not be plotting anyone's death, but perhaps your eyes have not seen the true value of someone else's life: calling someone a fool, thinking ill of the needy, saying horrible things to a loved one. And when we do this to others, we do it to Jesus too.

Jesus sees our eyes and knows our thoughts. He died for us, giving new life for all who believe.

Lord Jesus, forgive us for our murderous eyes. Thank You for willingly giving up Your life for our sake, that we may live forever. Help us care for the lives of those around us. Amen.

The Name of God

Read Psalm 145:14–16

The eyes of all look to You, and You give them their food
in due season. (Psalm 145:15)

It doesn't take much. The clink of dishes, the crinkle of a wrapper, the crackle of sizzling meat. Many a dog knows when a meal is being prepared. And oh, those eyes. They stare, they plead, they train on the person with the food—even when good manners prevent the pup from whimpering.

A beloved pet knows where to look for all it needs. Those trusting, hopeful eyes pay complete attention to the one who gives care.

We're not canines, but our four-legged friends give us a nice example of the way we can look to our Lord: focused, trusting, hope filled.

Do we ever ignore the One who gives us all we need? Do we "bite the hand" that feeds us? Sadly, we do. We do not thank God for His gifts. We do not pray to Him for our needs. We grumble against His care.

Yet our Lord still feeds us. He still loves us. And He forgives our unfaithfulness and reminds us to keep our eyes on Him for all good things.

Lord, thank You for all Your gifts. Train our eyes on You. Amen.

For They See

Read Matthew 13:10–17

But blessed are your eyes, for they see, and your ears, for they hear. (Matthew 13:16)

In the famous Disney movie *Mary Poppins*, sight becomes an important theme. Mary tells the children that some people can't see past the end of their nose. She doubts that their father will be able to see the older woman who sells food to the birds. The children are delighted when it appears that he does. However, he doesn't. He doesn't realize that feeding the birds actually feeds the woman who is selling the small bags of food.

So often, people believe that they see what is in front of them. So often, they do not.

People saw Jesus. They spoke with Him. They listened to Him. But they did not see that He is the Son of God. They did not hear that His words give healing, forgiveness, and eternal life.

As Christians, we have been given exceptional sight and hearing. We also have been given mouths and hands to be used in order that others may see and hear. Pray that your eyes and ears hear and see Jesus clearly every day. He sees and listens to you.

Holy Spirit, help our eyes to see and our ears to hear our Savior. Amen.

Marvelous

Read Matthew 21:41–42

This was the Lord's doing, and it is marvelous in our
eyes. (Matthew 21:42)

Marvelous and *marvel* are words that have been used in many popular shows and movies lately. But what does it mean to marvel at something marvelous? In order to marvel, someone must see something, truly behold it, and then be filled with wonder and amazement by it.

Do you know someone who marvels? This person stops when everyone else is walking.

"Look! Do you see the trees? They are so green and lush!"

"Wait! Take a look at that sweet little teacup. Can you imagine how someone could have made it?"

"Oh, what a delightful cupcake. Think of all the care that went into this."

"How can a sunset possibly be so stunning?"

What causes you to marvel? We all have seen something marvelous. In addition to our daily blessings, we have seen the Lord's work. We know of our Savior, our God, who gave His life for us. We know of His gifts, which give us life forever and ever and ever.

Can you fathom such a thing?

Lord Jesus, we marvel at Your merciful love for us. Help us share this wonder with all. Amen.

LENT
WEEK FIVE

See You Later

Read John 14:15–21

Yet a little while and the world will see Me no more,
but you will see Me. Because I live, you also will live.
(John 14:19)

See you later! For most of us, this phrase is a common, informal expression. Likely, this good-bye is not a particularly significant one.

Essentially, Jesus is saying this to His disciples in this passage, but it is by no means insignificant.

Jesus is saying several important things here.

1. He is going to die.
2. He is going to rise.
3. We will also die and rise.
4. We will see Him again.

This was one of the last times He would see His followers before He died for them. It was an incredibly important good-bye. "See you later" was a promise.

As believers, we are comforted knowing that we will see Jesus and all loved ones who rest in Him. On the day of resurrection, we will see Jesus with our very own physical eyes. In Jesus, we can always say, "See you later," no matter what.

Jesus, we look forward to the day we see You face-to-face. Amen.

He Sees

Read Psalm 94:9–15

He who formed the eye, does He not see? (Psalm 94:9)

Sometimes, it feels as if no one sees our troubles. We become indignant when we suffer injustice. Who will avenge us?

Sometimes, it feels as if no one sees our sins. We become prideful when we seem to get away with misdeeds. Who will discipline us?

God does both. He has created every eye, and He certainly can see all that goes on in His creation. Out of love, He disciplines those who are stuck in their sin so that they may turn to Him for forgiveness. He also sees when harm comes to those He loves, and He will give justice to the wicked.

In the most severe act of justice, our wages of sin—death—were paid, but not by us. By God Himself. Now that sin is paid for, justice is satisfied. Our death is no longer required of us for the sin we commit.

Instead, we can point to Jesus with confidence that we have nothing to fear. Instead, we turn to our God, who leads us according to His will and who protects us with His might and justice.

Lord Jesus, deliver us from our own sins and the sins against us. Amen.

Every Eye

Read Psalm 139:13–24; Revelation 1:4–8

Behold, He is coming with the clouds, and every eye will
see Him, even those who pierced Him, and all tribes of
the earth will wail on account of Him. Even so. Amen.
(Revelation 1:7)

Can you picture it? One day, in an instant, trumpets will call out, and every single person will see Jesus come—at the same time. For all who look to Him in faith, it will be a beautiful, wonderful, incredible day. For all who look to Him without faith, it will be the worst day of all.

It has been said that we should live as if it were our last day. It has been better said that we should live as if Jesus were coming back today.

What's the difference?

Well, if we are living in faith, our own personal death is a mere gateway to life, and there is nothing to fear.

But if we live as if it were the last day for everyone, then we will live with an urgency to tell others of Jesus, so that when they see Him, it will be with great joy.

Even so, we trust that God will use us according to His will as we eagerly tell all nations of His love.

Even so, come, Lord Jesus! Amen.

WORLDLY EYES

Read Mark 15:1–20

For [Pilate] perceived that it was out of envy that the
chief priests had delivered [Jesus] up. (Mark 15:10)

Even Pilate could see why Jesus was before him. The chief priests
were jealous of Jesus. They were so jealous that they wanted Him dead.

What a sad sight.

A governor sees the King of the universe in front of him and yet
fears the crowds.

Leaders see their long-awaited Messiah and yet only focus on their
temporary power.

The mob sees their Savior and yet only pay attention to the voices in
the crowd calling for death.

The soldiers see the One who will gain victory over death itself and
yet beat Him nearly to death.

What do we see when we look at Jesus? Do we see Him with worldly
eyes, only focusing on the Jesus we want Him to be? Or do we remember all that He has done and will do for us?

When Jesus looks at us, He sees His beloved ones, those He willingly died to save.

King of kings, have mercy on us. Amen.

My Eyes Have Seen

Read Luke 2:27–32

Lord, now You are letting Your servant depart in peace, according to Your word; for my eyes have seen Your salvation. (Luke 2:29–30)

We don't really know how old Simeon was, or how many days he had seen. But we do know what he was looking for. God promised him that he would see the long-awaited Savior before he died.

When he held Jesus in his arms, Simeon rejoiced. Likely with a sparkle in his eye, he proclaimed that Jesus was the Son whom God had promised. He told Mary that she would endure tragedy. He foretold that Jesus had come for all people.

And he prayed, holding God in his very hands. "Lord, . . . my eyes have seen Your salvation." Simeon may have died that night or many years later; we don't know. But Simeon was ready. God had kept His promise to him and to all people.

God keeps His promise to us. In Holy Communion, we hold our Savior in our hands, and we receive forgiveness. We may die later that day or many years later. Regardless, we go in peace, serving our Savior until He comes again.

Lord Jesus, thank You for coming to dwell with us, to come even into our own hands and into our hearts. Amen.

Seen and Heard

Read 1 John 1:1–3

That which we have seen and heard we proclaim also to
you, so that you too may have fellowship with us; and
indeed, our fellowship is with the Father and with His
Son Jesus Christ. (1 John 1:3)

When we see something amazing, we just have to tell someone. The
new restaurant, the great movie, the lovely park. The Savior of all? Why
wouldn't we share the news of Him?

John saw Jesus, and he spent the rest of his life proclaiming this
incredible Gospel to all he could. Why? So that others, too, will join
together with him and his brothers and sisters and his Brother and his
Father—united in the Spirit.

We are a part of that long line of people in fellowship with God and
one another, thanks to someone who has told us all that they have seen
and heard.

Who is next? Whom will you tell of all that you have seen and
heard?

What a joy it is for us to share the amazing news of grace, mercy,
forgiveness, peace, life (we could go on) found in Jesus.

Lord Jesus, I thank You that I am in fellowship with You. Amen.

Let Our Eyes Be Opened

Read Matthew 20:29–34

And stopping, Jesus called them and said, "What do you
want Me to do for you?" They said to Him, "Lord, let our
eyes be opened." (Matthew 20:32–33)

Two men with clear vision were sitting by the roadside as a crowd
of blind people followed Jesus.

Yes, you read that right. Jesus walked out of Jericho and toward Jerusalem. Two men knew that He was coming, and they called out to
Him for mercy.

The crowd, blind to the eyes of faith that these men had, rebuked
the two men. Surely Jesus had no time for people such as these.

Jesus saw them. He stopped, and He asked them for their request.

Suddenly, a great many eyes were opened when the two men and
the crowd witnessed a miracle of mercy that was given freely.

But they had seen nothing yet. Jesus was on His way to Jerusalem
for a reason. Very soon afterward, He would close His own eyes in death.

His eyes would not stay closed, however. His eyes would open
again, ensuring that all eyes would open once again. And those with
eyes of faith would live forever in a place where all would see perfectly.

**Lord Jesus, heal us from our eyes that do not always see You and
Your merciful love. Amen.**

HOLY WEEK

They Had Seen

Read Luke 19:28–40

The whole multitude of His disciples began to rejoice
and praise God with a loud voice for all the mighty
works that they had seen. (Luke 19:37)

Think of all the people who saw Jesus ride into Jerusalem on Palm Sunday.

The Pharisees and Sadducees saw a man on their "most wanted" list.

The guards saw someone who seemed capable of inciting an uprising.

The Romans saw a Jewish man who was evidently popular with the people.

The multitudes began to rejoice and praise God, for they had seen what Jesus could do. They had seen Him teach, heal, listen, welcome, rebuke, feed, comfort, bring to life, and do countless mighty works. For the disciples, there didn't seem to be anything Jesus couldn't do.

It can be hard to believe that just days later, He would be the beast of burden, carrying the cross—and so much more—to the hill where He would bear the weight of all the sin of the world and conquer our worst enemies.

Yes, they had seen Him perform all kinds of mighty works. But His mightiest work was yet to come.

Lord Jesus, we thank You for all of Your mighty works, especially Your work on the cross, carrying our sins to their death. Amen.

Flipping Tables

Read Mark 11:15–19

And the chief priests and the scribes heard it and were
seeking a way to destroy Him, for they feared Him,
because all the crowd was astonished at His teaching.
(Mark 11:18)

Flipping tables has almost become cliché on social media. Whenever someone is angry, they place an image of someone flipping a table. The implication is that this fury comes from righteous anger.

Most of the time, the anger displayed is anything but righteous. Jesus' anger, of course, was nothing but righteous.

It can be puzzling when sinners are met with the almighty righteousness of God. We don't understand how God's mind works—we are left astonished. Or like the chief priests, we are left in fear and very unrighteous anger.

The scribes and chief priests were seeking a way to kill Jesus because they could not—and did not want to—understand Jesus' teaching. Instead of listening and learning from God in their midst, they sought a way to be rid of Him.

We don't always like what God says. We want to think that we are more righteous than even God Himself, judging His judgments. Where do we think we know better than God?

We can complain all we want, but we are not God. We can either listen in amazement, or we can shut Him out of our lives. The thing is, ridding ourselves of Jesus is a pronouncement of death not on Jesus but on ourselves.

Look and see your Savior. He dies for you. He lives for you. He loves you, even when He has every right to be angry. Learn from Him whose wisdom has no end.

Lord Jesus, teach us Your ways. Amen.

TUESDAY IN HOLY WEEK

THE ARMS OF GOD

Read Revelation 21:3–5

He will wipe away every tear from their eyes, and death
shall be no more, neither shall there be mourning, nor
crying, nor pain anymore, for the former things have
passed away. (Revelation 21:4)

Shoes wear out. Clothes rip. Tires get holes. Knees get skinned. Hearts break. Tears fall.

These are just a part of our reality on this earth. They are so much a part of our reality that we forget that this is not the way that God designed our lives to be. We ruined it all with our sin, and now bees sting, rashes itch, friends fight, and everything dies.

God would not stand for this forever. This death simply could not reign without His intervention. So, God died.

God died.

All of creation is turned on its head when the Lord of Life gives up the life He has.

God rose.

God rose, taking up His life again and reversing all of death. There will come a day when nothing is dead, nothing will fade, nothing will hurt.

No tears will fall, for our Lord will reach down to His beloved children and wipe each tear away.

Lord of Life, we wait for You and the life You bring. Amen.

MISUNDERSTANDING

Read John 13:1–17

Jesus answered him, "What I am doing you do not
understand now, but afterward you will understand."
(John 13:7)

Poor Peter. Sometimes I wonder what he thought when he looked
back on his time with Jesus. "Oh, of course! I get it now."

Granted, Peter was still a sinner who surely had more misunderstandings. (In fact, we know this to be true.) But God also used him to
bring the lifesaving Gospel to countless others. (We know this to be true
as well.)

Jesus had a few hours left to teach His disciples before He would
be arrested. What did He do with that time? Among other things, He
washed their feet. He showed them selfless, unconditional, humble love.

"For I have given you an example, that you also should do just as I
have done to you" (v. 15).

Just like Peter, we will still fail and have misunderstandings. Just like
Peter, God will use us to show His love to others.

After Jesus died and rose and ascended and sent His Spirit, Peter
could understand more. The Helper lived inside of him and guided his
ways. The Holy Spirit lives in us too, and with His help, we can understand.

Holy Spirit, give us understanding. Amen.

HOLY THURSDAY

More Than Meets the Eye

Read Mark 14:22–24

This is My body. . . . This is My blood. (Mark 14:22, 24)

We will never fully understand it. We confess that the body and blood are in, with, and under the bread and wine.

As Paul wrote: "The cup of blessing that we bless, is it not a participation in the blood of Christ? The bread that we break, is it not a participation in the body of Christ?" (1 Corinthians 10:16).

We do not know how this is possible, but we believe it because Jesus said it is true. The mysteries of Holy Communion are amazing indeed.

It draws us into communion (fellowship) with all believers, in this world and the next.

It gives us forgiveness of sins.

It places Jesus in our very mouths.

It blesses us with strength for the days to come.

What an incredible gift! There is certainly more than meets the eye in this simple meal that comes to us with God's Word and by His command.

In this world, we will hear all kinds of things about what the Lord's Supper is and is not. We trust the words of Jesus Himself and wait for the day when He returns and He dwells with us again.

Lord Jesus, give me eyes of faith to see what I cannot see on my own. Amen.

THE BLOOD OF GOD

Read Mark 15:21–39

And when the centurion, who stood facing Him, saw
that in this way He breathed His last, he said, "Truly this
man was the Son of God!" (Mark 15:39)

Throughout this season, many have been reflecting on the eyes of
God through song. As we contemplate eyes during Lent, we focus both
on how we see Jesus and also how He sees us. Whether or not you've
been singing these words, take time today to consider them.

Our eyes behold the Savior's face
And yet cannot perceive
That His perspective held our grace
Before we could believe.

Our focus flits and fails to see
The One whose steadfast gaze
Propelled Him to the darkened tree
Enveloped in death's haze.

Our sights train on the dreadful cross.
Beneath His knowing eyes,
Our sins are bare and set for loss;
He sees us as His prize.

Our vision blurs with anxious tears
As Jesus' eyelids fall
To conquer sin and all our fears
And tear in two our pall.

Our view scans for the coming Day
That evermore grows near,
When Jesus wipes our tears away
And all is crystal clear.

Lord Jesus, I thank You for seeing me as Your beloved. Amen.

Resting Eyes

Read Mark 15:40–16:1

Mary Magdalene and Mary the mother of Joses saw
where He was laid. (Mark 15:47)

Jesus had what we might call an epic day. He carried the sins of the world. He suffered the worst of everything. His Father forsook Him. He gave up His Spirit.

And He, God Himself, died.

He paid the price. He faced the devil and sin and death. He obeyed perfectly. He descended into hell and proclaimed victory in Satan's own capital.

He won.

In just a few hours, all would know what the devil knew: Jesus had died, and He would rise, and there was nothing that would stop Him.

But on Saturday, His body rested. There was much more to do the next day.

Mary and Mary saw where the tomb was, and they would be among the first to know . . .

Lord of Life, give us rest in You. Amen.

THE RISEN BODY OF GOD

Read Mark 16:1–8

Do not be alarmed. You seek Jesus of Nazareth, who
was crucified. He has risen; He is not here. See the place
where they laid Him. (Mark 16:6)

It must have been a great delight to be on guard duty. For the angel,
that is.

The angels had seen it all: the fall of the devil, the fall of creation, the
Son dwelling on earth, His death, and now—now, the moment that all
creation had been waiting for.

An angel waited for the women who sought Jesus. And this holy
messenger was able to tell the message for the first time:

"He is not here."

Did you notice that no one during Jesus' day actually claimed that
Jesus was still in His tomb? No Romans, no Jewish leaders, no unbe-
lievers. They made all kinds of claims, but they all knew what the angel
proclaimed:

"He is not here."

No, Jesus was not there. He was risen and victorious, and He was
going to celebrate the very first Easter with His beloved followers, that
they might see with their own eyes and know that He truly was their
living Savior.

Risen Lord Jesus, let us see with faith what we know to be true:
You are risen! Keep us in Your care till the day when we see Your
risen body with our own risen bodies. Amen.